COUNTRY

Formal Name: Kingdom of Saudi Arabia (Al Mamlakah al Arabiyah as Suudiyah).

Short Form: Saudi Arabia.

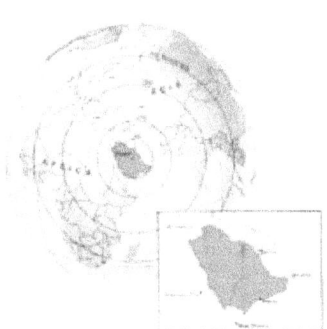

Click to Enlarge Image

Term for Citizen(s): Saudi Arabian(s) or Saudi(s).

Capital: Riyadh (estimated population 3.6 million).

Major Cities: Population estimates for 2006 show continued growth for Saudi Arabia's major urban areas: Jiddah (2.9 million), Mecca (1.6 million), Ad Dammam/Khobar/Dhahran (1.6 million), and Medina (854,500). Mecca and Medina have religious significance that far outweighs their respective populations.

Independence: Following Ottoman dominance, Egypt controlled Arabia from 1818 to 1824. For the remainder of the nineteenth century, Egypt, Britain, and the Ottomans vied for control of the region. On September 23, 1932, Abd al Aziz ibn Abd ar-Rahman Al Saud established the Kingdom of Saudi Arabia. Unification brought together competing tribes into a modern state, covering an area approximating present boundaries.

Public Holidays: In accordance with Wahhabi theology, Eid al Fitr and Eid al Adha are Saudi Arabia's only national holidays. Both holidays are dependent on the Islamic lunar calendar, and thus the dates of celebration vary from year to year. In recent years, Shia Muslims have been allowed to celebrate the holiday of Ashura in select cities of Eastern Province and in the south. Ashura is not, however, a national holiday. Saudis commemorate September 23 as their Independence Day.

Flag: The Saudi flag features white lettering on a green background. The Arabic text reads: "There is no god but God: Muhammad is the Messenger of God." Below the letters, also in white, is a sword.

Click to Enlarge Image

HISTORICAL BACKGROUND

Pre-Islamic Period: By 1000 B.C., southern Arabia had evolved significantly as a result of steady contact with the outside world via the trade routes that spanned the region. Exports in frankincense and myrrh brought wealth and global connections to present-day Bahrain, Yemen, Oman, and southern Saudi Arabia. While the Persians and Romans fought to control the Near East, Arab society benefited from the exchange of ideas that came with the camel caravans.

Multiple religions were present in the region, including Christianity, Judaism, and various polytheistic paganisms.

Early Islam: The birth of the Prophet Muhammad in A.D. 570 forever shaped Saudi Arabia. Today, many Arabs refer to the era before the introduction and spread of Islam as "the time of ignorance." Muhammad was born in the city of Mecca into the prominent Quraysh tribe. His life and ministry did much to unify Arabia. Until the seventh century, the peninsula's tribes fought a destructive series of wars for control of the region. The situation had changed dramatically by the time of Muhammad's death in A.D. 632. Muhammad, as well as his political successor Abu Bakr, enjoyed the loyalty of almost all of Arabia. Although the Prophet did not appoint a spiritual successor, the institution of the caliphate emerged and expanded the Islamic empire.

For the first 30 years following the Prophet's death, caliphs ruled the Islamic world from Yathrib, today known as Medina. Responding to threats from the Byzantine and Persian empires, the caliphs demanded allegiance from the Arab tribes. In a relatively short span of time, the Islamic empire expanded northward into present-day Spain, Pakistan, and the Middle East. However, maintaining unity proved to be a continual challenge. Following the death of the third caliph, Uthman, in 656, splits appeared in the burgeoning Islamic empire. The Umayyads (661–750) established a hereditary line of caliphs centered in Damascus. The Abbasids, claiming a different hereditary line, overthrew the Umayyads in 750 and moved the caliphate to Baghdad. Although the spiritual significance of Mecca and Medina remained constant, the political importance of Arabia in the Islamic world waned.

The Al Saud and Wahhabi Islam: The Al Saud family emerged as the dominant factor in Saudi Arabia's history. The clan's origins can be traced to Najd, near Riyadh, beginning in about 1500. As a small town developed, the Al Saud came to be recognized as its leaders, and the clan's power and influence grew. The rise of the Al Saud coincided with that of the Muslim scholar Muhammad ibn Abd al Wahhab (1703–87), who wrote and preached against leaders and traditions that he deemed contradictory to the idea of a unitary god. Unlike other religious leaders who preached unitarianism, Muhammad ibn Abd al Wahhab demanded that political power be used to implement his theology. In 1744 Muhammad ibn Abd al Wahhab found a political partner in Muhammad ibn Saud, and the two swore a traditional oath to work together in order to establish a state ruled according to Islamic principles. The alliance was based on Muhammad ibn Abd al Wahhab's claim of religious legitimacy and Muhammad ibn Saud's readiness to undertake jihad in defense of such principles. By 1765, Muhammad ibn Saud's forces had established Wahhabism and with it Al Saud political authority over most of Najd.

After Muhammad ibn Saud died in 1765, his son, Abd al Aziz, continued the Wahhabi advance. In 1802 the Al Saud–Wahhabi armies sacked Karbala, including the Shia shrine commemorating Husayn, the martyred grandson of the Prophet Muhammad whom Shia Muslims regard as their spiritual forefather. In 1803 Wahhabi forces moved on to Mecca and Medina. With the assault on the Hijaz, the region of pilgrimage, the Al Saud invited conflict with much of the rest of the Islamic world. Recognizing the symbolic importance of the region, the Ottoman sultan ordered the recapture of the Hijaz, and in 1812 and 1813 Egyptian forces, fighting on behalf of the sultan, regained control of Mecca and Medina. Meanwhile, Muhammad ibn Abd al Wahhab had died in 1792, and Abd al Aziz died shortly before the capture of Mecca.

Nineteenth-Century Arabia: Following a six-year period of Egyptian interference, the Al Saud regained political control of the Najd region in 1824 under Turki ibn Abd Allah, who rebuilt Riyadh and established it as the new center of Al Saud power. Although they did not control a centralized state, the Al Saud successfully controlled military resources, collected tribute, and resisted Egyptian attempts to regain a foothold in the region. From 1830 to 1891, the Al Saud maintained power and protected Arabia's autonomy by playing the British and Ottomans against each other. External threats were largely kept at bay, but internal strife plagued the Al Saud throughout much of the century. After the assassination of Turki in 1834, the family devolved into a series of competing factions. The infighting and constant civil war ultimately led to the decline of the Al Saud and the rise of the rival Al Rashid family; the Al Saud were driven out of Riyadh and forced to take refuge in Kuwait.

Establishing a Modern State: Abd al Aziz laid the groundwork for the modern state of Saudi Arabia while exiled in Kuwait. In 1902 he led a small force in a raid against the Al Rashid garrison in Riyadh, successfully gaining a foothold in Najd. From there, he cultivated his Wahhabi connections, establishing himself as the Al Saud leader and as a Wahhabi imam. During the next 25 years, Abd al Aziz gradually extended his authority. This slow process culminated in the conquest of the Hijaz in 1924. Thus, after nearly 40 years the Al Saud again controlled Islam's most holy land.

Unlike most other Arab countries, Saudi Arabia existed independent of Western control. That autonomy had been achieved in large part because of the military strength of the radical Ikhwan forces, desert warriors organized by Abd al Aziz and dedicated to promoting Wahhabi Islam. With victory achieved, the Ikhwan expected a strictly Wahhabi state. Ultimately, however, Abd al Aziz moved to rein in the Ikhwan. He assembled a diverse and committed political coalition and was able to maintain a delicate political balance between religion and modernization. The Kingdom of Saudi Arabia became an official state in 1932 and subsequently faced severe economic constriction in the 1930s. Fortunately, however, following the worldwide depression, geologists made a discovery that significantly buoyed the region's economic outlook—enormous and easy-to-access deposits of oil.

Abd al Aziz's Successors: Following Abd al Aziz's death in 1953, Saud succeeded his father as king in a reign largely characterized by wasteful state expenditures and the polarization of wealth. In 1964 the royal family and ulama, responding to public discontent, deposed Saud and appointed his half-brother Faisal as king. King Faisal aggressively pursued modernization, introduced Western technology, and increased public education. His reign (1964–75) witnessed increasing diplomatic complexity both within the Arab world and beyond its borders. When conflict broke out in the Middle East, Saudi Arabia remained on the periphery. In 1967 Saudi Arabia claimed neutrality during the Six-Day War between Arab and Israeli forces. During the 1973 Arab-Israeli conflict, Saudi Arabia again decided not to participate militarily, but it did join the Arab oil boycott of the United States.

External conflicts were coupled with internal threats. In 1975 Faisal fell victim to an assassination plot carried out by one of his nephews. The assassin was only one member of a larger group of discontented royal family members. Although ultimately it was determined that the assassin acted alone, the threat of internal strife loomed over the kingdom, now led by

Faisal's half-brother Khalid. In 1979 internal revolt once again reared up in Saudi Arabia, as 500 dissidents seized the Grand Mosque in Mecca, claiming that Saudi Arabia had abandoned its traditionalist roots in favor of Western corruption. After two weeks of careful planning, the Saudi military overtook the dissidents, and all of the surviving male radicals were beheaded. Far from discounting the dissidents, however, King Khalid made some effort to address their grievances.

Khalid's half-brother, Crown Prince Fahd, ascended the throne following Khalid's death after a short illness in June 1982. The crash of oil prices in 1986 brought economic challenges to the entire Middle East region. Saudi Arabia functioned as a stabilizing force in the region throughout the turbulent 1980s. King Fahd played an important role in bringing about a cease-fire between Iraq and Iran in August 1988. He also supported the formation and strengthening of the Gulf Cooperation Council (GCC), an alliance of the six Persian Gulf states of the Arabian Peninsula, with headquarters in Riyadh. The Gulf War in 1991 changed regional diplomatic relationships significantly. Faced with the threat of Iraqi imperialism following Iraq's invasion of Kuwait, Saudi Arabia requested the assistance of the United States and a multinational coalition to defend the Saudi border, and King Fahd played a pivotal role in bringing together Western allies with GCC and other Islamic states. Throughout the 1990s, Saudi Arabia's diplomatic and economic relationship with the United States remained strong. But, while proving advantageous to Saudi Arabia's global position, it aroused criticism in the Arab world and exposed Saudi Arabia to the ire of radical Islamists. Nevertheless, widespread oil prosperity defused many regional tensions.

King Fahd, who had proved to be an effective leader capable of instituting liberal reforms and strengthening bonds among Arab countries, suffered a massive stroke in 1995. He survived, but with limited capacities. His half-brother, Crown Prince Abd Allah (Abdullah), served as the de facto ruler of Saudi Arabia until formally becoming king upon King Fahd's death on August 1, 2005. King Abd Allah has served effectively in the face of continuing external and internal challenges, including terrorism, Islamic extremism, regional instability, and burgeoning domestic unrest. In particular, the attacks on the United States on September 11, 2001, brought unwanted attention to the Saudi connection to terrorism, given that 15 of the 19 hijackers were Saudis. The Saudi government has, for the most part, cooperated with the United States in fighting the spread of terrorism and Islamic extremism in the region. Its traditional ties to the United States have grown closer as a result of increased U.S. emphasis on security over political reform in Saudi Arabia since the September 11 attacks.

Democratic Reforms: Since 1995, Saudi Arabia has made subtle changes in its governance structure. Concerns over balancing the various factions of the royal family led to the creation of new advisory groups and a slight diffusion of power. In 2003 the government announced a reorganization of the Council of Ministers and then plans to create municipal councils and to hold democratic elections. Originally scheduled for October 2004, the first stage of the municipal elections finally took place February 10, 2005. In general, the candidates exhibited far more enthusiasm than the voters. More than 1,800 candidates sought election to 592 seats, but only about 25 percent of eligible male voters (and possibly as few as 15–20 percent) cast votes. While some observers viewed the elections as a mark of progress, critics concluded that the poor turnout reflected a general dissatisfaction with the limited extent of the legislative reforms.

GEOGRAPHY

Location: Saudi Arabia is located in the Middle East, occupying about 80 percent of the Arabian Peninsula.

Click to Enlarge Image

Size: Saudi Arabia has a land area of 1,960,582 square kilometers according to U.S. government statistics. Saudi figures, however, denote a land area of 2,250,000 square kilometers. Either way, Saudi Arabia is approximately one-fifth the size of the United States.

Land Boundaries: Saudi Arabia has a total of 4,431 kilometers of borders with Yemen (1,458 kilometers), Iraq (814 kilometers), Jordan (744 kilometers), Oman (676 kilometers), the United Arab Emirates (457 kilometers), Kuwait (222 kilometers), and Qatar (60 kilometers).

Disputed Territory: Only portions of the border with Yemen, demarcated in 1934, are clearly defined. The discovery of new oil repositories in the 1990s led to border disputes between Saudi Arabia and both Yemen and Jordan, some of which were resolved in the early 1990s. Additionally, Saudi Arabia and Kuwait share two Divided Zones, one administered by each country, along their short border. The zones contain about 5 billion barrels of proven oil reserves. Saudi Arabia and Kuwait have allowed foreign countries to operate oil fields in the zones while taking an equal share of the revenues.

Length of Coastline: Saudi Arabia has 2,640 kilometers of coastline—nearly 1,800 kilometers along the Gulf of Aqaba and the Red Sea and the remainder along the Persian Gulf.

Maritime Claims: Saudi Arabia claims a territorial sea of 12 nautical miles and a contiguous zone of 18 nautical miles, as well as some small islands, seabed, and subsoils beyond the 12-nautical-mile limit.

Topography: The Arabian Peninsula is an ancient massif whose geologic structure developed concurrently with the Alps. Geologic movements caused the entire mass to tilt eastward and the western and southern edges to tilt upward. In the valley created by the fault, called the Great Rift, the Red Sea formed. On the Arabian Peninsula, the eastern line of the Great Rift fault is visible in the high escarpment that parallels the Red Sea between the Gulf of Aqaba and the Gulf of Aden. The eastern slope of the escarpment descends gradually. A second, lower escarpment, the Jabal Tuwayq, runs north to south through the area of Riyadh. In the south, a coastal plain rises gradually from the sea to the mountains. The southern region boasts the country's highest mountain ranges, reaching about 3,000 meters. The central plateau, Najd, extends east to the Jabal Tuwayq and slightly beyond. A long, narrow strip of desert separates Najd from eastern Arabia, which slopes eastward to the sandy coast along the Persian Gulf. North of Najd, a larger desert isolates the heart of the peninsula from the steppes of northern Arabia. South of Najd lies one of the largest sand deserts in the world, the Rub al Khali. Extensive coral reefs buttress much of Saudi Arabia's coastline, making natural ports rare.

Principal Rivers: Saudi Arabia has no permanent rivers or lakes. However, in eastern Arabia, artesian wells and springs provide valuable water resources. Additionally, in many areas of northern and eastern Arabia significant underground aquifers lie beneath the desert. The largest contains more water than the entire Persian Gulf.

Climate: The climate in Saudi Arabia differs greatly between the country's two distinct regions: the coast and the interior. High humidity coupled with more moderate temperatures is prevalent along the coast, whereas aridity and extreme temperatures characterize the interior. Temperatures along the coast rarely exceed 38° C. In the interior, mostly desert, the average daytime temperature in the summer is 45° C, but it is not uncommon for temperatures to reach 54° C. The capital, Riyadh, has an average temperature of 42° C in July and 14° C in January. Temperatures rarely drop below freezing. Most of Saudi Arabia receives only infrequent rainfall. However, the southwestern province of Asir experiences monsoons between May and October, bringing an average of 300 millimeters of precipitation.

Natural Resources: Saudi Arabia's vast oil resources have shaped the kingdom's development. The country also has large natural gas reserves, as well as deposits of bauxite, coal, copper, gold, iron, phosphates, platinum, silver, tungsten, uranium, and zinc. Non-mineral resources include limestone, glass sand, and stone.

Land Use: Most of Saudi Arabia consists of arid or semi-arid land. Uninhabitable desert covers nearly half the country. According to 2005 statistics, only 1.67 percent of Saudi land is classified as arable, and only 0.09 percent of the country's land is planted to permanent crops. Irrigated land totaled an estimated 16,200 square kilometers in 1998. In the more temperate regions of the kingdom, adequate forage exists to support cattle grazing.

Environmental Factors: Saudi Arabia faces numerous environmental challenges. The country has very little arable land. Water scarcity is a constant concern, as are the related issues of desertification and creeping sands. The region's dryness results in frequent dust and sand storms that can cripple transportation. The lack of perennial rivers or permanent bodies of water poses a continual challenge, as does the depletion of underground water resources. Additionally, coastal oil spills, though infrequent, contribute to pollution.

Time Zone: Saudi Arabia operates on Greenwich Mean Time plus 3 hours.

SOCIETY

Population: In July 2006, estimates placed Saudi Arabia's population at 27,019,731, with an annual growth rate of 2.18 percent. The population total includes nearly 6 million non-nationals. Approximately 100,000 foreigners enter the country each year, mostly to fill specific job openings. Immigrant workers come primarily from other Arab and Muslim countries, including many from South Asia and the Philippines. Fewer than 100,000 Westerners work and live in Saudi Arabia. Because most of the terrain is unsuitable for cultivation, the coastal areas and interior oases support the vast majority of the population. Some cities have reported densities of 1,000 people per square kilometer. The Mecca region, which also contains the major city of Jiddah, is the most populated area of the country, with nearly 26 percent of the total population. Other population centers include Riyadh and the clustered Eastern Province cities of Ad

Dammam, Khobar, and Dhahran. The least populated regions lie at the kingdom's periphery, to the extreme north and south.

Demography: Saudi Arabia has an overwhelmingly young population. According to 2006 estimates, 38.2 percent of Saudis are under the age of 15, 59.4 percent are 15–64 years of age, and only 2.4 percent are 65 and older. The median age for males is 22.9, for females 19.4. The sex ratio is 1.2 males/female. The birthrate and death rate are estimated to be 29.34 per 1,000 and 2.58 per 1,000, respectively. Saudi Arabia has a relatively low infant mortality rate, estimated to be 13.7 deaths per 1,000 live births. It has a relatively high level of life expectancy: 73.66 years for males and 77.78 years for females, or 75.67 years overall. The country's fertility rate is 4.1 children per woman, a significant drop in the past 20 years from 6.4 births per woman in 1985.

Ethnic Groups and Languages: Saudi Arabia's population is very homogeneous. The native population is 90 percent Arab and 10 percent Afro-Asian. Arabic is the official language.

Religion: Islam is the official religion of Saudi Arabia. Islamic law forms the basis for the country's legal code, and all citizens must be Muslim. Eighty-five percent of Saudis are Sunni Muslims, most adhering to the Wahhabi sect. About 2 million Shia Muslims live in Saudi Arabia, primarily in the east. The presence of religions besides Islam results almost exclusively from the presence of foreign nationals, including a sizable number of Hindus and Christians. The U.S. Conference of Catholic Bishops has estimated that between 500,000 and 1 million Catholics currently reside in Saudi Arabia. In recent years, the Saudi government has stated a policy of allowing non-Muslim foreigners to practice their religion privately, but no change in the law reflects this sentiment. Public worship of other religions is prohibited by law and regulated and punished by the state's Committees for the Propagation of Virtue and Prevention of Vice. Proselytizing by non-Muslims and by non-Sunni Muslims is strictly prohibited. Conversion from Wahhabi Islam to another religion is a crime. The government controls all mosques and is the direct employer of imams. It also operates centers designed to facilitate the conversion of foreigners to Islam. Non-Sunni Muslims are largely eliminated from consideration for government employment and educational opportunities.

Education and Literacy: The U.S. Department of State estimates the Saudi literacy rate to be 84.7 percent for males and 77.8 percent for females. Saudi Arabia's nationwide public education system includes eight public universities and more than 20,000 schools. Public education—from elementary through high school—is a major government priority and is open and free to every citizen. In 2005 the government devoted 25 percent of total expenditures to education. Parents are not, however, required to send their children to school. Estimates from 2001 suggest that 59 percent of age-relevant children enroll in primary education. About 61 percent of those eligible attend intermediate and secondary schools, according to 1996 data. Education remains closely tied to Islamic teachings. All curricula must conform to Islamic laws and the Quran, and traditional gender roles still limit the educational opportunities available to females. The education of females has increased dramatically in recent years, from 25 percent of all students in 1970 to 47.5 percent in 2001. However, classroom instruction remains strictly segregated. Additionally, women can only attend six of the nation's eight universities, and they are prohibited from studying certain subjects. Whereas men may travel to foreign countries to pursue education, women are discouraged from doing so and generally must be accompanied by a spouse or male relative.

Health: Health benefits for Saudi citizens have increased exponentially since the implementation of the first five-year development plan in 1970. Today, according to the Saudi government, every citizen has access to unlimited, free medical care. The government provides the bulk of financing to build and operate hospitals throughout the country. As of 2006, the Saudi Ministry of Health operated 62 percent of the country's hospitals and 53 percent of its nonurgent-care centers. Expenditures for health and social services account for about 13 percent of the government's 2006 budget. Although spending has increased, management problems have hindered coordination among the various state, private, and military health care providers.

Saudi Arabia has a two-tiered health care system. A series of clinics, many of them mobile units that serve the country's remote rural towns, provide minor and preventative health care. Most of the doctors in the country are not Saudi—only about 20 percent according to recent estimates. Government officials expect this number to increase as education for doctors improves in the country. Saudi Arabia's medical advances can be seen clearly in the increasing number of specialized service providers. As recently as 1980, most Saudi hospitals provided only general medical care, but in May 2006 Saudi Arabia terminated its long-standing practice of sending patients to the United States for more complicated procedures. Government attention instead has focused on continuing to improve Saudi facilities and expertise.

Statistics indicate a relatively high level of health in Saudi Arabia. According to 2002 estimates, there are 1.5 doctors and 2.3 hospital beds per 1,000 persons. Nearly the entire Saudi population has access to sanitation, and 95 percent of Saudis have access to clean water. Similarly, nearly 100 percent of the population has access to affordable essential drugs. The immunization rate for children approaches 100 percent. For example, immunization against tuberculosis and measles has increased to 94 percent of all one-year-olds. Of births occurring in 2002, 91 percent were attended by a trained health professional.

The Saudi government does not release comprehensive health statistics, but United Nations estimates on human immunodeficiency virus and acquired immune deficiency syndrome (HIV/AIDS) for 2006 place the adult prevalence rate at less than 0.02 percent. Since 1985, Saudi Arabia has nearly eradicated diphtheria, poliomyelitis, whooping cough, and measles. Tuberculosis and hepatitis B have proved more difficult to eliminate. The health status of women and children has attracted some concern from international organizations. Health workers report that physical spousal abuse and violence against women and children appear to be common problems. A 2003 report by the Saudi Ministry of Interior estimated that 21 percent of females suffered some form of abuse. To address this problem, the Saudi government has now mandated that hospitals report any suspicions of violence against women, domestic or otherwise, to law enforcement officials.

Welfare: Among developing nations, as categorized by the United Nations in 2005, Saudi Arabia ranks thirty-second out of 103 countries on the Human Poverty Index (an assessment of standard of living), ahead of most of its Middle East neighbors, and seventy-seventh out of 177 nations on the Human Development Index (a comparative measure of well-being and child welfare). Through its series of five-year development plans, Saudi Arabia continues to try to transform oil wealth into broader economic prosperity. But despite high oil prices and rising oil production, the average Saudi's standard of living has fallen, and unemployment, especially among young adults, continues to rise. Moreover, the perception that oil revenues are not equitably distributed throughout the population continues to create some social discontent.

Saudi Arabia's General Organization for Social Insurance, a semi-state body, was established in 1969. A 9 percent payroll tax funds social insurance programs. Saudi businesses and individuals are also responsible to the Ministry of Finance for the *zakat* (almsgiving), the Islamic tithe of 2.5 percent of one's net worth. Old-age pensions are paid to retired workers at a rate of 2.5 percent of the last average salary. Men must be 60 years of age and women 55 in order to begin receiving payments. Additionally, all Saudis are granted a plot of land and a small loan to build a house.

ECONOMY

Overview: Saudi Arabia has a robust economy that experienced rapid growth from 2003 to 2005 but remains largely dependent on the production and exportation of oil. Saudi Arabia produces more oil and natural gas liquids than any other country in the world. The Saudi Arabia Oil Company (Saudi Aramco), which was fully nationalized in 1988, controls this vitally important resource. Even as the demand for oil, and consequently the price per barrel, remain at historic highs, Saudi Arabia faces the challenge of diversifying its economy. In 1999 a royal decree established the Supreme Economic Council under the leadership of the crown price and charged it with bringing Saudi Arabia's economy into the twenty-first century. Since the 1970s, the Saudi government has used five-year development plans to try to make its economy less susceptible to fluctuations in oil prices. Currently in its eighth five-year plan (2005–8), the government has goals of achieving modest but consistent gross domestic product (GDP) growth, increasing the role of the private sector in the economy, and creating significant numbers of new jobs for Saudi citizens.

Despite ambitious government plans for economic modernization and diversification, the development of the non-oil economy has proceeded slowly, and attempts in the past decade to encourage private investment have been hampered by the many vested interests of the royal family, which continues to dominate the economy. Strong oil sales have boosted government revenues and enabled robust government spending (a trend expected to continue in the near term), but analysts note a long-term decline in national living standards. Compared to some other oil-dominant economies, such as the United Arab Emirates and Kuwait, Saudi Arabia has a relatively low per capita GDP. Popular discontent has been rising for years among Saudi citizens who feel that not enough of the country's oil wealth goes back to the people. Although production has boomed, there is actually less oil money to go around. Saudi Arabia's per capita oil export revenue in 2004, US$4,500 per person, was far less than the high of nearly US$23,000 reached in 1980. Economic discontent will likely continue to reverberate as high levels of unemployment plague the country's young male population.

Gross Domestic Product (GDP): According to estimates, Saudi Arabia's gross domestic product (GDP) will reach between US$308 billion and US$338 billion in 2005. Should these estimates prove accurate, the total would represent a healthy increase over the US$215 billion to US$251 billion posted in 2003 and 2004. Estimated per capita GDP was US$12,800 in 2005. Projections for future GDP growth remain bright: 5.4 percent for 2006 and 4.6 percent for 2007, following high annual growth rates of 7.7 percent, 5.2 percent, and 7.5 percent, respectively, in 2003–5. Oil prices and production will undoubtedly determine the validity of such forecasting.

Government Budget: Since 2002, when oil revenues began to increase dramatically, Saudi Arabia has produced large budgetary surpluses. Before that time, high defense spending and government subsidies to consumers, coupled with low oil production rates and prices, generally yielded significant budgetary deficits. Saudi Arabia's 2006 budget includes government spending of nearly US$90 billion, a 20 percent increase over 2005. This plan will continue the government's strategy of using record oil revenues to provide broad economic stimulus. Government spending priorities include education, health and social affairs, municipal services, transportation, and infrastructure. Even with its ambitious spending plans, the government projects a budget surplus of US$15 billion in 2006, based on estimated 2006 revenues of US$104 billion. About 20 percent of revenue will be from non-oil income. Government officials expect tariff and duty revenue to decrease as the full effects of Saudi Arabia's ascension to the World Trade Organization are borne out.

Because of the significance of oil revenue, Saudi Arabia imposes only minimal income taxes on Saudis and does not have a capital gains or value-added tax, although a payroll tax supports social insurance programs, and the government collects the Islamic tithe of 2.5 percent of net worth from both businesses and individuals. Joint ventures and non-Saudi individuals and businesses are taxed at varying rates.

Inflation: Saudi Arabia controls internal inflation through a series of price subsidies. When necessary or expedient, the government intervenes to drive market prices down for consumers. For example, in April 2006 the government slashed automobile gas prices by 20 percent. Externally, however, the weak U.S. dollar, to which the riyal is pegged, continues to drive up the cost of imported goods. According to the cost of living index calculated by Saudi authorities, consumer prices rose by 1.1 percent in 2005. Inflation is expected to remain very low in the kingdom at between 0.4 and 0.5 percent through 2006.

Agriculture, Forestry, and Fishing: The agriculture sector accounted for 4 percent of Saudi Arabia's 2004 gross domestic product (GDP), down from 5.1 percent in 2002. Agriculture employs about 6 percent of working citizens. The scarcity of water and fertile soil limits the crops that can be grown. The principal crop in recent years has been wheat. In 2003 Saudi farmers produced more than twice as much wheat as any other agricultural commodity. Other significant crops include dates, potatoes, tomatoes, watermelons, and sorghum. Saudi Arabia is self-sufficient in the production of most dairy products. Saudi agriculturalists annually produce a surplus of eggs and broiler chickens. Nearly 75 percent of the country's land is still used for low-grade grazing of livestock rather than for cultivation. This has led the Ministry of Agriculture to establish a research center dedicated to finding the most efficient and profitable means of utilizing and protecting pastureland.

According to Saudi estimates, the country possesses nearly 6 million acres of forested land, but this area cannot sustain a forestry industry. The Saudi government has taken measures in recent years to conserve existing forests. It set up 20 nurseries across the country to cultivate seedlings and produce fertilizers and planted tree barriers along the edges of selected forests in order to guard against creeping sand and desertification. The fishing industry, through capture and aquaculture, produced an annual catch of 55,000 metric tons in 2002.

Mining and Minerals: Extraction efforts in Saudi Abaia focus on petroleum and natural gas. According to the U.S. Energy Information Administration, oil makes up 90–95 percent of Saudi Arabia's exports, 70–80 percent of state revenues, and about 40 percent of the country's GDP. Despite its economic clout, however, the oil industry employs only 1.5 percent of the working population. Government-controlled Saudi Aramco, the world's largest producer of petroleum, facilitates the oil industry in Saudi Arabia and in fact dominates the entire mining industry. Moreover, the company's influence and role in overall economic planning and performance cannot be overstated.

Saudi Arabia has proven oil reserves of more than 261.9 billion barrels, which will allow continued production at present rates (nearly 11 million barrels per day in 2005) for about 50 years. In order to control prices and guard against glutting the world market, Saudi Arabia adheres to the quotas set by the Organization of the Petroleum Exporting Countries (OPEC), of which it is an influential member. Saudi Aramco officials claim that oil production could be ramped up to 15 million barrels per day if the market justified such an expansion. The country's oil infrastructure has grown rapidly, doubling the number of drilling rigs in the country (90), between 2004 and 2006. Nevertheless, challenges still lie ahead, including guarding against the threat of terrorism and addressing the decline of oil fields. A typical decline rate of 5–12 percent annually means that Saudi Arabia must boost production by 500,000 to 1 million barrels daily just to maintain current output.

In addition to oil, Saudi Arabia has large deposits of natural gas—235 trillion cubic feet, the fourth largest natural gas reserves in the world, representing nearly 4 percent of the world's total natural gas reserves. In 2002 Saudi Arabia completed construction on the world's largest natural gas plant, located in Hawiya. Saudi officials hope that the plant will increase production by up to 30 percent. Iron ore, gold, and copper also are major mining industries. On a smaller scale, the extraction of limestone, gypsum, marble, and clay augment the mining industry's annual output.

Industry and Manufacturing: Manufacturing in 2004 contributed 8.8 percent of gross domestic product (GDP) and in 2002 provided employment to 8.1 percent of the Saudi workforce. Experts projected a manufacturing production growth rate of 7.1 percent for 2005. Most manufacturing jobs are tied in some manner to the minerals sector. Refining petroleum continues to be the most important activity. In 2005 Saudi Aramco increased production of refined products by 3 percent. Cement production rose by 2 percent. Additionally, the manufacturing of fertilizer and steel contribute significantly to the country's economy. Ship repair, commercial airline repair, and construction also provide the region with much-needed industrial jobs.

Energy: Most of the country's electric energy comes from thermal power stations, which use the country's petroleum resources. Additionally, electricity produced through the desalinization of seawater has become increasingly important in the past decade. Saudi Arabia produced 145.1 billion kilowatt-hours of electricity while consuming only 134.9 billion kilowatt-hours in 2003. Demand for electricity has expanded as a result of the country's growing population and artificially low consumer prices (as a result of government subsidies). According to the Ministry of Industry and Mining, the demand for electric power grows by 7 percent a year; thus, further expansion of electricity production will be needed. The government has taken steps to encourage private investment in this sector in order to meet the exorbitant cost of such rapid growth.

In the 1970s, the government pushed for consolidation in the energy sector, and small, private companies were merged as a result. In 1998 government consolidated the producers of electricity even further, creating a public company, the Saudi Electric Company, with shares for purchase on the stock market. This government control did not last, however. In order to expand the energy grid to include all regions of the country (currently 20 percent of Saudis are not served by the national grid) and to meet future needs, the Saudi government has eased restrictions on Independent Power Producers (IPPs) and Independent Water and Power Projects (IWPPs). The recently completed Ghazlan II power project was the first in Saudi history to receive a significant portion of its funding from an international commercial loan (US$500 million of the US$1.7 billion total cost of the project). The Saudi government plans to establish 10 IWPPS by 2016.

Services: The services sector produced 44.1 percent of the gross domestic product (GDP) in 2002 and employed 73 percent of the workforce. In 2005 it produced an estimated 35–38 percent of GDP. According to a 2002 survey of the services sector, 16 percent of Saudis worked in retail, 12 percent in education, and 10 percent in domestic service.

Banking and Finance: Saudi Arabia has a profitable and stable banking industry, closely regulated by the Saudi Arabia Monetary Fund (SAMA). Saudi banks that conform to Islamic law prohibiting interest payments have the benefit of not paying their depositors to hold their money. This, along with high oil revenues, has led to high profits for Saudi banks in recent years. SAMA reported that total bank deposits reached US$138 billion in the first quarter of 2006. SAMA estimates that non-performing loans comprise only about 9 percent of the banking industry's lending portfolio. No bank has ever failed in Saudi Arabia.

The banking sector is composed of 13 Saudi-owned banks and eight branches of foreign banks. The country's largest bank, the National Commercial Bank, is controlled by the Saudi government and operates under Islamic principles. Saudi Arabia only recently began opening its doors to foreign banks. The Gulf International Bank (Bahrain) arrived first in 2000, followed by the Emirates Bank International (United Arab Emirates), the National Bank of Kuwait, and the National Bank of Bahrain in 2002. The Capital Market Law, passed in 2003, eliminated further barriers to foreign financial institutions. In addition to commercial banks, which meet general banking needs, five government-developed credit institutions are designed to meet private and corporate financing needs: the Real Estate Development Fund, established in 1974; the Saudi Industrial Development Fund; the Saudi Arabian Agricultural Bank, which was founded in 1964; the Public Investment Fund, which lends to "commercially oriented public corporations;" and the Saudi Credit Bank, established in 1971 to make personal loans to low-income Saudi citizens for marriage expenses, vocational training, and building projects. Besides commercial banks and the five government funds, only a few investment banks and other financial intermediaries exist. The venture capital and entrepreneur finance sectors of the economy remain underdeveloped, as most Saudis continue to rely on either family or friends to provide capital for business development. Insurance companies are in their infancy. Prior to passage of the Co-operative Insurance Companies Control Law of July 2003, the government had a monopoly on the insurance industry.

The Saudi stock market is the largest in the Arab world, with a total market capitalization valued at nearly US$650 billion at the end of fiscal year 2005, a 111 percent increase from one year prior. Established in 1990 by SAMA, Saudi Arabia's stock market only opened to investors outside the Gulf Cooperation Council (GCC) in 1997. Public interest and participation have increased during the past few boom years. Stocks, bonds, mutual funds, and initial public offerings (IPOs) have become common investment strategies for the country's financially aware citizens. In 2001 SAMA established an online trading system called Tadawul that made securities more accessible. Additionally, the Capital Market Law of 2003 established an official trading floor for the Saudi Arabia Stock Exchange. Still, the legacies of corporate secrecy and government interference in business remain stumbling blocks to wide participation in the securities market. Moreover, the decline of the stock market in February 2006 after three years of record gains provided a sobering warning to investors.

Tourism: Saudi Arabia is aggressively pushing the development of its tourist industry. The secretary general of the Tourism Higher Authority (THA) boldly predicted that Saudi Arabia would have 45.3 million tourists in 2020. Presently the THA has embarked on an aggressive expansion of tourist facilities. An estimated 4.8 million tourists came to Saudi Arabia in 1999, generating receipts of more than US$1.4 billion. The World Tourism Organization estimated that in 2004 Saudi Arabia received 8.6 million visitors who spent a combined total of US$6.5 billion.

The hajj is the bedrock of Saudi tourism. In 2004 nearly 2 million pilgrims came to Saudi Arabia. Additionally, nearly 500,000 Saudis take part in hajj activities each year. Currently, expansion projects are underway in order to increase the number of pilgrims that can be accommodated. Outside of the hajj period, visitors performing the *omra*, or minor pilgrimage, visit Mecca and Medina. Until recently, these pilgrims were restricted to the primary religious cities. However, in 2000 the government approved tourist visas that would permit further travel in the kingdom, and travel companies can now conduct group tours, although restrictions on who can enter the country remain in effect. Significant barriers to tourism still exist for non-Muslims, although Saudi Arabia initiated a pilot program of granting tourist visas in early 2006.

Since non-hajj tourism has never been a significant industry in Saudi Arabia, many tourist-friendly operations that other countries take for granted are not in place. To begin rectifying this situation, the Supreme Commission for Tourism has proposed instituting a hotel rating system, developing roadside rest areas, funding hotels in rural regions, encouraging archeological and museum visitors, and licensing tourist companies. The commission has also developed plans for expanding education opportunities for those interested in the hospitality and hotel industries.

Labor: Labor, or rather sufficient employment, is a significant problem in Saudi Arabia. The unemployment rate has risen to nearly 25 percent (estimates vary from 13 percent by the Saudi government to 25 percent by the U.S. government), and the economy remains dependent on the skills and expertise provided by the 6 million foreign nationals residing in the country. Current estimates place the workforce in Saudi Arabia at 6.76 million, with foreign workers constituting nearly one-third of that total. Resolution No. 50, passed in 1995, required that the workforce of any company with more than 20 employees be at least 5 percent Saudi. This requirement was raised to 10 percent in 1999. Additionally, in 2001 the Saudi government prohibited the awarding of contracts to companies not complying with Saudiization and stipulated that foreign workers applying to change jobs would be charged a fee.

Saudi Arabia does not have a minimum wage, but most workers earn a wage adequate to meet their family's basic needs. Overtime must be paid for hours worked beyond the federally mandated 48-hour workweek. The government prohibits the formation of labor unions and collective bargaining, although it has begun to allow the establishment in larger companies of "labor committees," whose members must be approved by the Ministry of Labor and Social Affairs.

Numerous reports exist of maltreatment of workers in Saudi Arabia. Charges include forced labor, martial punishment, and using trafficking victims to meet labor needs. Foreign workers are particularly vulnerable to exploitation because contracts generally favor employers, and reporting a grievance to the labor courts often takes months. The government offers arbitration services between workers and employers in cases of alleged abuse.

Foreign Economic Relations: Because of its massive oil revenues, Saudi Arabia regularly produces a significant trade surplus. The country's major trade partners are Japan, the United States, and the European Union. Saudi Arabia maintains memberships in most of the region's economic organizations, including the Cooperation Council for the Arab States of the Gulf, Islamic Development Bank, Organization of Arab Petroleum Exporting Countries, and Organization of the Petroleum Exporting Countries. Saudi Arabia became the 149th member of the World Trade Organization (WTO) in December 2005, evidence that it is making strides toward market modernization.

Saudi Arabia maintains a close economic relationship with the United States and other oil-consuming nations. The United States, followed by Japan, South Korea, and China, receives the majority of Saudi exports. In 2004 the United States was both the leading market for Saudi exports and the leading supplier of imports, as it had been in previous years. Japan also does significant business with Saudi Arabia. In addition to trade connections, the Saudi riyal is pegged to the U.S. dollar. Thus, when U.S. officials adjust monetary or fiscal policy, Saudi leaders typically follow suit.

Imports: Increasing demands for consumer goods in Saudi Arabia have driven up overall imports in the kingdom, a trend that is expected to continue for the foreseeable future. The total value of imported goods in 2006 is expected to increase from the estimated total of US$51 billion in 2005. The largest categories of imported goods are machinery and vehicles, which make up about 50 percent of all imports, as well as appliances, electrical equipment, sound and television apparatus, aircraft, and cars. The United States continues to be Saudi Arabia's leading source of imports (13 percent in 2005). Imports from the United States include military equipment, machinery, foodstuffs, and transport equipment. European countries, including Germany, France, and Britain, are other leading suppliers.

Exports: Nearly 90 percent of Saudi exports are related to oil. Petrochemicals, plastics, construction materials (cement especially), and agricultural products make up the remainder of Saudi exports. Export earnings (mainly from oil and petroleum products) totaled an estimated US$175 billion in 2005. The value of exports is expected to increase in 2006, as increased production likely will offset any reduction in the price of oil. The United States and Japan receive the largest share of Saudi exported commodities—about 17 and 14 percent, respectively, of the 2005 total. Other primary destinations include South Korea, China, Singapore, and Taiwan.

Trade Balance: Saudi Arabia annually produces a significant trade surplus. Even in the wake of the 1973 oil shock, revenues from exports exceeded the cost of imports. Saudi Arabia posted a trade surplus of nearly US$124 billion in 2005, almost solely the result of a banner year for oil production and prices.

Balance of Payments: Saudi Arabia's significant trade surplus in goods is offset by deficits in the exchange of services and investment. In contrast to the goods sector, Saudi Arabia annually experiences a trade deficit in the services sector. The Saudi Arabian Monetary Agency (SAMA) projects that the country will experience a deficit of US$35.8 billion for services and transfers in 2005. On average, Saudi Arabia spends about four times as much on importing foreign services as it receives from foreign entities purchasing Saudi services. Nevertheless, overall Saudi Arabia has enjoyed a positive balance of payments over the past few years. The country last recorded a negative balance of payments in 1998. For 2005 SAMA recorded a record US$90 billion current account balance.

External Debt: In 2005 Saudi Arabia's public debt was an estimated $38.78 billion, or approximately 11 percent of gross domestic product. Saudi Arabia maintains about US$27 billion in reserves of foreign exchange and gold.

Foreign Investment: As a result of the improving climate for foreign investment in Saudi Arabia and sustained high oil prices, foreign direct investment has boomed since 2000. After years of rhetoric without substantial change, Saudi Arabia made its first real allowances to foreign investors with the Foreign Investment Act of 2000. The law guaranteed foreigners protection against Saudi nationalization of particular industries and reduced the income tax on foreigners. The Capital Market Law of 2003 created further opportunities, allowing for initial public offerings and denationalizing some industries. In 2004 Saudi Arabia received about US$300 million in foreign direct investment. According to the Saudi Arabian General Investment Authority (SAGIA), investment capital secured through investment licenses increased 787 percent in the first quarter of 2005 over the same quarter in 2004. Despite these advances, foreign investors have been hesitant to participate in Saudi ventures because of the long tradition of government interference in the marketplace, bureaucratic nuisances, and concerns about instability and terrorism. Moreover, the government continues to ban foreign investment in national defense or certain sectors with religious significance such as health and pilgrimage services.

The acceptance of foreign capital in Saudi Arabia has made it easier for foreign businesses to follow. Foreign companies, however, face a distinct disadvantage in terms of taxes. Saudi-owned businesses pay only the *zakat* (a 2.5 percent alms tax) on company assets and property while foreign-owned companies face a tax rate of up to 20 percent (or even as high as 80 percent in the hydrocarbon sector). Restrictions on the Saudi stock exchange have reinforced the government's prominent role in economic development and discouraged foreign investors. The Saudi stock exchange is now partially open to foreign investors, but trading remains limited. Non-Gulf Cooperation Council citizens can only invest in Saudi Arabia's equity market by purchasing mutual funds managed by Saudi banks. Foreign investment in the Saudi stock market probably will not become widespread until foreigners can purchase stocks and equities directly.

With the collapse, beginning in 1998, of the Saudi government's National Gas Initiative, which sought to free up crude oil for export by locating new gas supplies to meet domestic needs, a distinct opportunity has emerged for foreign investors in the gas sector. International oil companies, including the U.S. firm Chevron Texaco, have been allowed to pursue a number of "upstream" gas development sites. Additionally, the Saudi government has recently opened the insurance, education, pipeline services, and mobile telephone sectors to foreign investment. The government also has tried, with limited success, to force its largest foreign investors to disperse their money more widely in the Saudi economy. The Saudi offset program mandates that companies with large military and, in some cases, commercial contracts invest a portion of their profits in Saudi industries.

Foreign Aid: Saudi Arabia gives aid to less affluent nations, primarily Arab and other Muslim states. In 1974 a royal decree established the Saudi Fund for Development (SFD), which provides grants and loans to developing countries. Specifically, the SFD supports the export of non-crude-oil commodities by providing the financing to get such operations underway. According to the Saudi government, 68 different nations have been party to 369 SFD loan agreements. Saudi officials also claim that assistance to poor countries has at times reached as high as 6 percent of Saudi Arabia's gross national product and that the country has given more than US$20 million to developing Islamic countries in the past 15 years.

Not surprisingly, Saudi Arabia has given more generously during times of high oil revenues. Since 2000, Saudi officials have earmarked the following aid packages: Palestine (US$307 million), Iraq (US$1 billion in loans and export guarantees, US$133 in grants), and Pakistan (US$153 million for earthquake recovery).

Currency and Exchange Rate: Saudi Arabia's currency, the riyal (SAR), is pegged to the U.S. dollar. Therefore, the rate in terms of U.S. value remains stable: SAR3.75=US$1.

Fiscal Year: Saudi Arabia's fiscal year coincides with the calendar year.

TRANSPORTATION AND TELECOMMUNICATIONS

Overview: Once accessible only via camel caravan, Saudi Arabia has made rapid improvements in its transportation and communications networks through its five-year development plans. Improvements in roads, railroads, airports, and telecommunications have come rapidly since 1970. However, with agricultural and industrial development, traffic also has increased rapidly. Continuing improvements will be necessary to allow for long-term economic growth as well as to decrease congestion and preserve the quality of urban life.

Roads: Saudi Arabia is served by more than 156,000 kilometers of roads, about one-third of which are paved and the rest, improved earth. This network is vital not only for use by private citizens, but also to allow the oil industry to grow and prosper. The Trans-Arabian Highway serves to link Saudi Arabia's major cities—Ad Dammam, Riyadh, Jiddah, Mecca, and Medina. Most villages in Saudi Arabia, even in remote areas, are now connected to the larger road network. The road system also has connected Saudi Arabia more closely to its neighbors, both literally and diplomatically. The King Fahd Causeway (known also as the Bahrain Causeway), completed in 1986, connects Saudi Arabia to Bahrain. Whereas the emphasis has largely shifted to maintaining the network of roads already in place, one future project under consideration is a causeway that would link Saudi Arabia to Egypt.

Railroads: As of 2004, Saudi Arabia had 1,392 kilometers of railroads, all at a standard 1.435-meter gauge. In 2001, 790,000 passengers traveled on Saudi trains. In addition, Saudi trains carried 1.5 million tons of cargo. In comparison to the other means of transport in the country, however, railroads remain relatively undeveloped. The difficult terrain has made laying track a costly endeavor. Currently, the country's most significant railroad is one that covers 570 kilometers between Riyadh and Ad Dammam, linking the capital with a significant port and industrial city. The Saudi Railways Organization (SRO), which oversees the country's rail network, has gained approval from the Supreme Economic Council for two major expansions that will add nearly 3,000 kilometers to the rail network. The Saudi Landbridge project will connect the port cities of Jiddah, Al Damman, Al Jubayl, and Riyadh with a modern rail system useful for both cargo and passenger transport. The Mecca–Medina Rail Link will connect Saudi Arabia's two holiest cities, making the transport of pilgrims more efficient and safe.

Ports: Saudi Arabia has 21 modern ports that handled 132 million tons of cargo and welcomed more than 1 million passengers in 2005. The major Red Sea ports are located in Jiddah, Yanbu, and Jizan. On the Persian Gulf, Ad Dammam and Al Jubayl are Saudi Arabia's most significant ports. In 2004 the industrial ports at Al Jubayl, Jiddah, and Yanbu each handled more than 30 million tons of cargo. Together, they handled more than 80 percent of the kingdom's cargo. The Jiddah Islamic Port, as it is officially titled, also serves as the main entry port for pilgrims arriving to visit Mecca and Medina. The port at Ad Dammam, like the one in Jiddah, has a fully equipped repair yard. The newest major port to be completed, located at the northern end of the Red Sea at Dhiba, is the closest port to the Suez Canal and Egyptian ports. The Saudi government, through its port authority, regulates all ports. As in most sectors of the economy, privatization is being attempted at a gradual pace. In 1999 some of the service aspects of port operation, including maintenance and management of docks, were opened to private contracts.

Inland Waterways: Saudi Arabia has no permanent rivers or waterways.

Civil Aviation and Airports: According to U.S. government statistics, Saudi Arabia has a total of 202 airports including 73 with paved runways and 129 with unpaved runways. The country also boasts six heliports. Saudi Arabia has four major international airports, located in Jiddah, Riyadh, Al Hufuf, and Dhahran. King Abd al Aziz International Airport serves Jiddah and currently handles about 13 million passengers annually. Plans exist for expansion in Jiddah to include a Hajj Terminal to further accommodate Muslim pilgrims. King Khalid International Airport serves the capital city of Riyadh. It currently has the capacity to handle 7.5 million passengers annually, but there are plans for expansion. A system of 24 regional airports connects the remote regions of the country to the international airports and consequently to the rest of the world. Currently, Saudi Arabian Airlines is the major operator for the region. With a fleet of more than 100 aircraft, it transports more than 10 million passengers annually and is the largest airline company in the Middle East.

Pipelines: According to U.S. estimates, Saudi Arabia has a total of 9,413 kilometers of pipeline. This total includes pipeline designated for condensate, 212 kilometers; gas, 1,780 kilometers; liquid petroleum, 1,191 kilometers; oil, 5,068 kilometers, and other refined products, 1,162 kilometers.

Telecommunications: In 1998 Saudi Arabia's telecommunications industry was largely privatized. The sector is now dominated by the Saudi Telecommunications Company, which employs more than 70,000 Saudis. The Ministry of Telecommunications and Information Technology provides governmental oversight.

Statistics gathered in 1998 showed that there were 43 AM, 31 FM, and two short-wave radio stations in operation in Saudi Arabia, and Saudis owned about 6.3 million radios (in 1997). Currently, two television channels broadcast in Saudi Arabia—one in English and one in Arabic, with 117 stations providing coverage throughout the country. Estimates from 2000 show that Saudis had 5.7 million television sets.

Saudi Arabia has a modern and expanding telephone system, with more than 3.6 million main lines in use in 2004. The technology used for domestic lines includes microwave radio relay, coaxial cable, and fiber-optic cable stems. Seven "earth stations" are linked to the Intelstat Satellite System, which allows Saudi citizens direct dialing access to more than 200 countries around the globe. According to 2002 statistics, Saudi Arabia had 151 telephone mainlines per 1,000 people. Mobile and cellular phones have become increasingly popular in the last decade. More than 9 million Saudis had cellular phones in 2004.

The use of personal computers and the Internet has increased rapidly in the early 2000s. Internet service first became available in Saudi Arabia in 1999. With access routed through a state server, the government, as it has in many industries, took control of the technological and economic development of the Internet. The number of Internet users in the country nearly doubled between 2003 and 2005, reaching 2.5 million.

GOVERNMENT AND POLITICS

Political System: Although some democratic reforms have been implemented, Saudi Arabia still operates as a near-absolute monarchy. Elections in 2005 for the first time allowed Saudi male citizens to choose municipal representatives. Very low voter turnout and skepticism about the elected officials' real power, however, have tempered any discussion of the development of unfettered democracy in Saudi Arabia. Nevertheless, the king does not have unfettered power. The Basic Law established in 1993 articulates the government's rights and regulations and sets forth the civil rights, system of government, and administrative divisions by which the state is run. Foremost, the Basic Law mandates that Islamic Law must come before all other considerations. The Quran and sunna (Islamic custom and practice based on Muhammad's words and deeds) are the state's constitution, and both the government and the society as a whole dismiss the notion that separation should exist between church and state. The king must not only respect Islamic law and tradition but also build consensus among members of the royal family and religious leaders (the ulama). He can be removed if a majority of the royal family calls for his ouster. The assumption of the throne by King Abd Allah (Abdullah) following the death of King Fahd on August 1, 2005, proceeded seamlessly. King Fahd's lengthy illness following an incapacitating stroke in 1995 and Abd Allah's tenure as crown prince undoubtedly facilitated the succession, defusing any potential conflict among vying factions of the royal family.

Succession in Saudi Arabia has proceeded smoothly during the country's short history, following the pattern set by Abd al Aziz of appointing an heir apparent as crown prince and first deputy prime minister. Since 1975 Saudi monarchs have also appointed a second deputy prime minister to serve as next in line on the unofficial succession slate. While other Middle Eastern countries such as Bahrain, Jordan, and Qatar have recently experienced a generational transfer of leadership, Saudi Arabia still has drawn only from among the sons of King Abd al Aziz in designating a ruler. As a result, Saudi leaders are taking the throne at a more and more advanced age. King Abd Allah and his half-brother Crown Prince Sultan are both between 75 and 90 years old. Because of their ages, the choice of a second deputy prime minister among Abd al Aziz's six remaining sons has increased significance, but King Abd Allah has thus far chosen to leave the position of second deputy prime minister vacant. Succession in Saudi Arabia will only become more challenging as the pool of potential candidates expands. The Basic Law clarified that the king must come from the Al Saud family, but once beyond Abd al Aziz's sons and grandsons, the number of possible kings will expand well into the thousands. Fractures within the royal family could form between reformists and traditionalists.

The Council of Ministers, created in 1953, is responsible for drafting legislation to be presented to the king. The council acts upon majority decision, but laws become official only with the king's decree. All legislation must be in accordance with Islamic law. The Council of Ministers includes a prime minister (the king), a first and second deputy prime minister, 23 ministers with portfolio (including the second deputy prime minister, who also serves as a minister), and five ministers of state.

In addition to the Council of Ministers, the Consultative Council serves at the king's pleasure. Following its inception in 1993, King Fahd restructured the council in 1997 and 2001 to expand the number of councilors. Currently, 120 councilors serve four-year terms. The king must approve all members. Most of the members are individuals with ties to the Al Saud family and tribal leaders, but the body also includes businessmen, academics, and some religious leaders. The consultative body has no power to act independently but it is empowered to hold debates, initiate investigative hearings, and enforce government-sponsored legislation. Since 2003, the Consultative Council has been increasingly included in the process of creating legislation.

The royal family dominates government and politics in Saudi Arabia. The family's vast numbers (hundreds in the main family alone) allow it to control most of the kingdom's important posts. Most members of the Council of Ministers and provincial governors come from the royal family. The increasing power of the Consultative Council represents a threat to royal family power, even though the king has largely supported its development. The possibility of electing half of the council, as proposed by some reformers, would further dilute the power of the royal family. Currently, the royal family remains firmly entrenched in power, but popular discontent has been building for years.

Administrative Divisions: A royal decree put forth in 1993 divided the kingdom into 13 provinces (*mintiqat*; sing., *mintiqah*): Al Bahah, Al Hudud ash Shamaliyah, Al Jawf, Al Madinah, Al Qasim, Ar Riyad, Ash Sharqiyah (Eastern Province), Asir, Hail, Jizan, Makkah, Najran, and Tabuk. A royal decree issued in 1994 subdivided the 13 provinces into 103 governorates.

Provincial and Local Government: In 1993 the king determined that a system of provincial government should exist. Subsequently, officials divided the country into 13 provinces, each of which was placed under the jurisdiction of a governor, usually a prince or close relative of the royal family. Four times each year, each governor meets with his provincial council to evaluate the province's development and make recommendations to the Council of Ministers regarding the province's needs. In October 2003, it was announced that 178 municipal councils would be created to advise the provincial governors. One-half of the new municipal council members were to be elected through universal male suffrage and one-half appointed by the central government. After numerous delays, the first of a planned three phases of elections took place in February 2005. Voter turnout reportedly was only about 25 percent or possibly even lower (15–20 percent) according to unofficial estimates. Numerous candidates, however, emerged. More than 1,800 candidates competed for a total of 592 seats on the 178 municipal councils. In Riyadh alone, more than 600 candidates competed for seven seats. The second phase took place in March 2005 in the Eastern, Asir, Jizan, Najran, and Al Bahah provinces. Low voter turnout again undercut the effort. Only 12 percent of eligible men voted. The final stage of the elections was held in April 2005.

The role of municipal councils is both to carry out on a local level the resolutions passed by the Council of Ministers and to mitigate regional concerns. According to the Basic Law, every citizen has the right to address his concerns with either the king or a royal prince. The king and princes hold open meetings for public discussion, as do municipal and regional leaders. The democratic election of some of those leaders will for the first time give Saudis a more direct voice in their government.

Judicial and Legal System: In contrast to its legislative branch, Saudi Arabia's judicial branch operates on a mostly independent basis, as stipulated in the Basic Law. However, members of the royal family are exempt from appearing before the courts, and allies of the family have received preferential treatment from judges in the past. Before the modernization of the judicial system in 1928, the system was severely fragmented among various judges who adhered to one of four schools of Islamic theology. After "unification," all courts were mandated to use the Quran and sunna as the basis for judgments without being limited to a particular school. Over time, some secular codes have been introduced to augment Islamic law.

The Ministry of Justice was created in 1970 to further unify the kingdom's vast system of courts and judges. In the same year, King Faisal formed the Supreme Judicial Council, with the responsibility of overseeing the court system and reviewing legal decisions. The Supreme Judicial Council assumed the task of approving all death, amputation, and stoning sentences. As of 2005, these forms of punishment had decreased in frequency, but they still exist. The king may grant pardons at his discretion, except to felons convicted of killing another individual. In this instance, the king must gain the approval of the victim's next of kin to grant a pardon.

A hierarchical court system allows the accused a process of appeal. The Ministry of Justice oversees the entire system. The General Courts, also referred to as the Courts of First Instance, are the first to hear cases and make decisions. The decisions of these courts may be appealed to the Supreme Judicial Council. Further appeals may be made to the Council of Ministers, but any decision of the council, signed by the king, is final. The law prohibits imprisonment for more than three days without being charged with a crime. There are reports, however, that this law has been ignored, especially by the religious police. According to the sharia, the court system should not give the testimony of a woman the same weight as that of a man. Additionally, a judge may throw out the testimony of non-Muslims.

A military justice system exists to try all members of the military and those persons accused of violating military regulations. The minister of defense and king review all decisions made by the military court.

Electoral System: Saudi Arabia had no history of electoral government until February 2005, when, in an election open only to male voters age 21 and older, Saudi citizens cast votes to select one-half the members of the municipal councils. The three-stage elections, which continued in March and April 2005, represented a fundamental step away from Saudi Arabia's absolute monarchy. There are also signs that a portion of the Consultative Council might be chosen via election in the near future. In general, the expanding power of the Consultative Council, in comparison to the traditional dominance of the Council of Ministers, is a positive sign for liberal reformers in the kingdom hoping for increased popular sovereignty. Nevertheless, out of a population of nearly 27 million, only about 3 million (males only) are eligible to vote. Women do not yet have the right to vote.

Politics and Political Parties: Political parties are illegal in Saudi Arabia, but distinct political divisions exist. Members of the royal family fill most of the important political positions in the kingdom, and the king and the Al Saud family rule by consensus. The ulama, a large and powerful group of religious leaders, perhaps numbering 10,000, ensure that the king observes

Islamic law above all other considerations. In order to placate the powerful religious majority of Saudi society, the Al Saud pays close attention to the interests espoused by religious leaders. Saudi Arabia's history of tribal organization also plays into the kingdom's political mix. Leaders of the principal tribes still command respect and authority. The traditional merchant families of Saudi Arabia also have a measure of political influence. The royal family has depended on the merchants at various times for financial support, and merchant revenues continue to be a steady source of government income. Finally, the new class of Saudi professionals and technocrats, emerging as a result of increased privatization of the economy, has informal influence on government ministers. Petitions signed by members of this class have encouraged some reforms.

Mass Media: Newspapers are privately owned but are subsidized and regulated by the government. Because the Basic Law states that the media's role is to educate and inspire national unity, most popular grievances go unreported in Saudi Arabia. In recent years, however, the government has allowed some critical stories to be written by selected journalists. Although self-censorship continues to be a method of self-preservation for the nation's media outlets, government censorship seems to be decreasing, especially on journalistic inquiries into crime and terrorism.

The government owns and operates the radio and television companies in Saudi Arabia. Censors remove objectionable material deemed offensive by the standards of Islam, including references to pork, Christianity and other religions, alcohol, and sex. Saudi citizens, however, have greater access to previously banned television broadcasts than ever before. According to the U.S. State Department's annual report on human rights practices, several million Saudis have satellite dishes that allow them to receive foreign television stations. Additionally, government censorship of the Internet has proved difficult. Although government officials monitor Internet sites for material deemed pornographic, politically offensive, or anti-Islamic, Saudi Internet users can gain access to most sites by simply connecting through an alternative server. The government recently created an appeals process by which citizens can request that particular Web sites be unblocked.

Foreign Relations: Saudi Arabia has strong ties to the nations of the Middle East as well as to other Muslim states and developed nations such as the United States and Japan. As the guardian of Islam's holy places, Saudi Arabia hosts millions of pilgrims from neighboring Islamic countries annually. Additionally, the mutual concern over oil prices has led to cooperation among oil-producing countries in the Middle East. As one of the more affluent countries in the region, Saudi Arabia has pursued aid and development for less developed Arab and Muslim states. Although Saudi Arabia has, at different times, suspended diplomatic relations with Iran and Egypt, among others, it continues to play a dominant role in the region. Saudi Arabia has its strongest diplomatic relations in the region with other members of the Gulf Cooperation Council (GCC): Bahrain, Oman, and the United Arab Emirates (UAE). In 2005, however, relations between these countries cooled somewhat when Bahrain, Oman, and the UAE each signed individual trade agreements with the United States. Saudi Arabia argued that the GCC should negotiate corporately and that the individual agreements violated the GCC's external tariff treaty.

Saudi Arabia maintains a complex diplomatic position between the Middle East and the West. It has consistently sought to promote Arab unity, defend Arab and Islamic interests, and support a peaceful resolution of the Israeli-Palestinian conflict (insisting, however, that Israel must withdraw from the territories occupied in 1967). On the other hand, Saudi Arabia has been a partner with the West in economic endeavors and the war against terrorism. Some in the Arab world castigate Saudi Arabia for its continuing relationship with the United States, viewed as Israel's most ardent protector. When Saudi Arabia called for military assistance following the 1990 Iraqi invasion of Kuwait, Yemen, Jordan, and the Palestine Liberation Organization (PLO) refused to support the Saudi coalition. Not until five years after the Gulf War did Saudi Arabia normalize relations with the PLO or Jordan.

Saudi Arabia has attempted to play the role of peacemaker, with mixed results. In 1981 King Fahd offered a "land for peace" initiative designed to ease tensions between the PLO and Israel, and in 2002 Saudi officials issued an updated version of the proposal known as the "Arab peace plan." However, the Saudi initiative was sidetracked when the United States initiated its own "roadmap" for peace in 2003. In early 2005, Saudi Arabia pressured Syria to withdraw its forces from Lebanon and helped defuse a potentially violent situation. Regarding the election of Hamas extremists to the leadership of the Palestinian Authority (PA), Saudi Arabia has maintained diplomatic contact while urging that the new government honor former Palestinian agreements on Israel. Saudi Arabia has hinted that its aid to the PA will be contingent on continuation of a moderate stance. In July–August 2006, Saudi Arabia called on the United States to intervene in the conflict between Israel and Hezbollah forces in Lebanon.

Saudi Arabia's economic and security relationship with the United States remains strong but not without tension. The terrorist attack on the United States in September 2001 placed considerable strain on the relationship since Saudi Arabia had been one of only two governments to recognize the Taliban administration in Afghanistan, and 15 of the 19 hijackers were of Saudi descent. In the ensuing war on terrorism, criticisms have been traded over the handling of prisoners, U.S. press coverage of Saudi connections to and financing of terrorist organizations, and a civil lawsuit brought against the Saudi government by relatives of the victims of September 11. Even as tensions mounted between the United States and Saudi Arabia, terrorists carried out attacks on Western interests and targets in Saudi Arabia in response to Saudi cooperation with the United States. Although seen as soft toward the West in parts of the Middle East, King Abd Allah, then crown prince, condemned the U.S. war with Iraq and refused to commit Saudi troops.

Membership in International Organizations: After a lengthy waiting and reform period, Saudi Arabia gained full membership into the World Trade Organization in December 2005. Saudi Arabia also maintains membership in the United Nations (UN), most UN specialized agencies, and numerous other international organizations. Regionally, Saudi Arabia has fostered close ties to other Arab and Islamic states through memberships in the Arab Bureau of Education for the Gulf States, Arab Monetary Fund, Arab Sports Federation, Gulf Cooperation Council, Islamic Corporation for the Development of the Private Sector, League of Arab States, Muslim World League, Organization of Arab Petroleum Exporting Countries, Organization of the Islamic Conference, and Organization of the Petroleum Exporting Countries (OPEC). Saudi Arabia also has membership in the International Monetary Fund.

Major International Treaties: Saudi Arabia is a party to many significant treaties, including international agreements on Biodiversity, Biological Weapons, Chemical Weapons, Climate

Change, Conservation, Desertification, Endangered Species, Gas Warfare, Genocide, Hazardous Wastes, Law of the Sea, Nuclear Nonproliferation, Ozone Layer Protection, and Torture. Saudi Arabia is not a signatory to the Kyoto Protocol or to conventions on Traffic in Women and Children or Terrorism. In 2005 Saudi Arabia ratified the World Health Organization's first convention on tobacco control. Treaties in Saudi Arabia are confirmed by a royal decree.

NATIONAL SECURITY

Armed Forces Overview: Over the past decade, Saudi Arabia has devoted significant resources to improving its military. Flush with oil revenue, Saudi Arabia increased military spending in 2005 by 21 percent over the 2004 level. Military spending (US$25 billion) actually surpassed the budget allotment. The Saudi military consists of an army, air force, navy, air defense, and paramilitary forces with nearly 200,000 active-duty personnel. In 2005 the armed forces had the following personnel: army, 75,000; air force, 18,000; air defense, 16,000; and navy, 15,500 (including 3,000 marines). In addition, the Saudi Arabian National Guard had 75,000 active soldiers and 25,000 tribal levies.

Foreign Military Relations: Since the Cold War era, Saudi Arabia has been militarily aligned with the United States. Saudi Arabia sided with Iraq in the Iran–Iraq war, but King Fahd called for the United States to intervene when Iraq invaded Kuwait and threatened the Saudi border in 1991. The United States and Saudi Arabia led an international coalition of forces to victory over Iraq in the ensuing Gulf War. The United States had served as the primary arms provider for Saudi Arabia until Britain supplanted it in 1988. Following the Gulf War, however, the United States again emerged as Saudi Arabia's primary arms supplier. In 1998 U.S. military exports to Saudi Arabia totaled US$4.3 billion, making Saudi Arabia the leading importer of U.S. military goods. The United States and Saudi Arabia continue to share a common concern over the regional stability of the Middle East—for both security and economic reasons. There have, however, been tensions between U.S. and Saudi military objectives. Saudi Arabia severed diplomatic relations with the Taliban in 2001 following the terrorist attacks on the United States but later lambasted the U.S. decision to attack the country and refused U.S. requests to operate from Saudi soil. Saudi Arabia also declined to participate in the 2003 Iraq war.

Saudi Arabia also provides the home base, as well as personnel and resources, for a small contingent of Gulf Cooperation Council (GCC) troops. The GCC force, called the Peninsula Shield Force, numbers about 10,000 men but has suffered from lagging commitment from GCC members. Discrepancies over how to train, arm, and fund the outfit have limited progress.

External Threats: Following the 1991 Gulf War, Saddam Hussein's Baathist regime in Iraq represented the greatest military threat to Saudi Arabia. Thus, Saudi officials closely monitored the movements of Iraqi troops. In 1999 Saudi Arabia broke precedent by openly calling for Iraqis to topple their leader. When fighting came in 2003, however, Saudi Arabia insisted on maintaining its distance from the war against Iraq. With the fall of the Iraqi regime in 2003, new and more amorphous forces have emerged as those most threatening to Saudi security. Like the other Arab countries in the Middle East, Saudi Arabia regards Israel as an ever-increasing threat to the region. Although Saudi ties to the United States mitigate some fear of Israel, Saudi Arabia has been active in pursuing a resolution to the Israeli-Palestinian conflict.

Iran is also a source of concern among Saudi officials in view of its military strength, potential nuclear capabilities, ties to Hezbollah and other radical Shia Islamists, alleged meddling in Iraq's civil unrest, and growing political influence in the region. Additionally, Saudi officials view the largely uncontrolled migration of tribesmen back and forth across the border from Yemen as a potential security risk. Relations between Saudi Arabia and Yemen suffered fromYemen's refusal to join the Gulf War coalition against Iraq and from a long-standing border dispute. A border agreement reached in 2000 lessened the tension between Saudi Arabia and Yemen significantly, but the porous border continues to elicit concern among Saudi defense officials.

Defense Budget: Spending on military and security forces totaled about US$25.4 billion in 2005. Saudi Arabia ranks among the top 10 in the world in government spending for its military. Military expenditures represent about 7 percent of gross domestic product (GDP), down from 10 percent in 2002. It seems likely that military expenses will continue to increase in the coming years. Because Saudi Arabia imports most of its military arms and equipment, the Saudi economy derives little benefit from growth of the defense sector.

Major Military Units: The Saudi military is divided into army, air force, navy, and air defense forces. The Saudi marines serve as part of the navy. The army is organized into three armored brigades, five mechanized brigades, one airborne brigade, one Royal Guard brigade, and eight artillery battalions. The army also has one aviation command with two aviation brigades. The navy is divided into two fleets with Naval Forces Headquarters in Riyadh. The Western Fleet has bases in Jiddah (Headquarters), Jizan, and Al Wajh. The Eastern Fleet has bases in Al Jubayl (Headquarters), Ad Dammam, Ras al Mishab, and Ras al Ghar. The marines are organized into one infantry regiment with two battalions. Saudi Arabia has at least 15 active military airfields. The air force is organized in seven fighter/ground-attack squadrons, six fighter squadrons, and seven training squadrons. The National Guard, augmented by 25,000 tribal levies, is organized into three mechanized infantry brigades, five infantry brigades, and one ceremonial cavalry squadron.

Major Military Equipment: Saudi Arabia ranks among the world's most densely armed nations, and it has ambitious plans to further upgrade its arsenal. In 2005 Saudi Arabia entered into an agreement with Britain to purchase 72 Eurofighter Typhoon fighter planes to replace its outdated Tornado planes. Additionally, Saudi Arabia plans to strengthen its National Guard by purchasing US$1 billion worth of armored vehicles from the United States.

The military already possesses a modern arsenal. The army's main equipment consists of a combination of French- and U.S.-made armored vehicles. According to the International Institute of Strategic Studies, the army is equipped with 315 M–1A2 Abrams, 290 AMX–30, and 450 M60A3 main battle tanks, many of which are in store; 300 reconnaissance vehicles; 570+ AMX–10P and 400 M–2 Bradley armored infantry fighting vehicles; 3,000+ armored personnel carriers, including the Al-Fahd, produced in Saudi Arabia; 200+ towed artillery pieces; 110 self-propelled artillery pieces; 60 multiple rocket launchers; 400 mortars; 10 surface-to-surface missiles; about 2,000 antitank guided weapons; about 200 rocket launchers; 450 recoilless launchers; 12 attack helicopters; 50+ transport helicopters; and 1,000 surface-to-air missiles.

The navy's inventory includes 11 principal surface combatants, 65 patrol and coastal combatants, 7 mine warfare vessels, 8 amphibious craft, and 7 support and miscellaneous craft. Naval aviation forces have 19 helicopters (armed) serving in naval support.

The air force has a fleet of nearly 300 combat aircraft but no armed helicopters. However, its operational capabilities are believed to have fallen considerably since the Gulf War. The fighter planes owned by the kingdom are primarily outdated F–5 models. After oil prices rose in 1999, Saudi officials began to look at purchasing more F–15 models. Increased internal security risks, however, diverted the funds that would have been necessary for such acquisitions. Currently Saudi Arabia has 291 combat aircraft, but most are nearing obsolete status. If Saudi Arabia's proposed purchase of British planes goes through, Saudi air power will be effectively modernized.

Military Service: The Saudi military is an all-volunteer force. Females do not serve in the military.

Paramilitary Forces: Saudi Arabia's paramilitary forces number more than 15,000 men, with 10,500 active troops in the Frontier Force and 4,500 in the Coast Guard, which is based at Azizam. Saudi Arabia also has a Special Security Force with 500 personnel.

Foreign Military Forces: Before the 9/11 attacks on the United States, about 5,000 U.S. military personnel, mostly air force, were stationed in Saudi Arabia. During 2003, the U.S. military redeployed most of its forces to Qatar. As of 2005, the United States has about 300 troops in Saudi Arabia. Saudi Arabia also provides a base for the 10,000 troops of the Peninsula Shield Force, the fledgling multinational force created by the Gulf Cooperation Council.

Military Forces Abroad: Although Saudi Arabia maintains an extensive military infrastructure within its borders, it has a policy of avoiding the foreign deployment of its troops except as required to protect the kingdom's direct security.

Police: The police force is controlled by the central government through the Ministry of Interior. The Saudi Arabia National Guard contributes significantly to security efforts. The Committees for the Propagation of Virtue and Prevention of Vice are the nation's religious police, which enforce compliance with religious laws.

Internal Threats: Neither petty crime nor organized crime is a problem in Saudi Arabia, although comprehensive statistics are not available. However, Saudi Arabia's quest to be both a modern and Islamic country has long aroused unrest. Connections to the West have caused some factions to call for the overthrow of the Al Saud ruling establishment. Minority groups of the left and the right seek to have more influence in the nation's governance. High unemployment and a generation of young males filled with contempt toward the West pose a significant threat to Saudi stability. Additionally, the Shiite minority, located primarily in the Eastern Province, has created civil disturbances in the past and could do so again. The government reportedly has expressed concern that instability in Iraq might promote restiveness among Saudi Arabia's Shia population. The presence of more than 6 million foreign workers also is thought by some to represent a threat to national stability. Finally, terrorist attacks in Saudi Arabia have made it clear that Saudi Arabia does harbor indigenous terrorists with probable ties to al Qaeda and other terrorist organizations.

An attack on Saudi Arabia's most productive oil complex in February 2006 renewed concerns about protecting the country's most valuable industry. Protection of the vital oil industry has long been and continues to be a priority. Saudi Aramco employs nearly 5,000 security personnel to guard its oil facilities, and both the Saudi National Guard and the Saudi military frequently are called upon to guard oil-producing facilities and pipelines.

Terrorism: Since the June 1996 attack by Iranian-backed terrorists on a Saudi military housing complex that killed 19 U.S. military personnel and wounded 500 people including 372 Americans, the Saudi government has increased efforts to fight terrorist elements within its own borders. The Saudi army has been successful in detaining several key militant/terrorist leaders. However, a series of bombings in 2003, an attack on the U.S. consulate in Jiddah and two car bombings in Riyadh in December 2004, and a February 2006 attack on an oil complex are evidence that elements linked to al Qaeda are present. Osama bin Laden was born in Saudi Arabia, and 15 of the hijackers carrying out the September 11 attacks were Saudi citizens. Recruitment of Saudi militants to engage in jihad against the United States and the West will likely continue.

Saudi Arabia does not openly support terrorist groups, but the United States has expressed concerns about Saudi financial ties to terrorism. Islamic networks originating in Saudi Arabia reportedly provide financial backing for terrorist groups that operate in the Middle East and around the world. The fact that many militant groups are mosque-based makes crackdowns difficult, but Saudi leaders have now accepted the need to control militant Islamist elements in the country. Moreover, officials have acknowledged that violence-inciting mosques and radical clerics cannot be ignored in the fight against terrorism. In February 2005, Saudi Arabia hosted its first-ever Counter-Terrorism International Conference. The government also began a public relations campaign discouraging religious radicalism and terrorism.

Human Rights: The U.S. State Department annual report on human rights is critical of several aspects of Saudi society. The report notes the lack of elected officials or political parties and the almost unlimited power of the king. Municipal elections have not abated concerns that the royal family holds too much power. The report finds that internal security forces have committed various human rights offenses, including torture and abuse of detainees, arbitrary arrests, and intimidation of non-Muslims and foreigners. The legal code permits corporal punishment, such as flogging, as well as amputation, stoning, and execution by beheading, although the use of such punishments reportedly has declined.

Freedom of speech and press are severely restricted in Saudi Arabia, although some reforms are underway. The government owns the country's television and radio companies and heavily subsidizes the country's newspapers. Both in law and practice, the Saudi government makes little pretext of providing freedom of religion. Non-Muslims may only practice their religions in private, and conversion from Islam to another religion is illegal, punishable in theory, if not in recent practice, by execution. The rights of women are improving, but they are still far from equal to those of men. For example, women cannot drive or travel without a male family member, and women must demonstrate significant cause in order to obtain a divorce while men are not required to do so. Women still face discrimination when entering non-traditional fields of employment and frequently are segregated from their male co-workers. Women were not permitted to vote in the recent municipal elections. The Basic Law does not guarantee the right to assemble, and the Saudi Government strictly limits the practice.